THINGS THAT STING

Killer Bees

By Sarah Machajewski

Gareth Stevens PUBLISHING

Please visit our website, www.garethstevens.com. For a free color catalog of all our high-quality books, call toll free 1-800-542-2595 or fax 1-877-542-2596.

Library of Congress Cataloging-in-Publication Data

Machajewski, Sarah, author.
Killer bees / Sarah Machajewski.
pages cm. — (Things that sting!)
Includes bibliographical references and index.
ISBN 978-1-4824-1707-4 (pbk.)
ISBN 978-1-4824-1708-1 (6 pack)
ISBN 978-1-4824-1706-7 (library binding)
1. Africanized honeybee—Juvenile literature. 2. Bees—Juvenile literature. I. Title.

QL568.A6M148 2015
595.79'9—dc23

2014026087

First Edition

Published in 2016 by
Gareth Stevens Publishing
111 East 14th Street, Suite 349
New York, NY 10003

Designer: Nicholas Domiano
Editor: Kristen Rajczak

Photo credits: Cover, p. 1 X-etra/Shutterstock.com; title texture: Asya Alexandrova/Shutterstock.com; caption box: VectorShots/Shutterstock.com; p. 5 Villiers Steyn/Shutterstock.com; p. 7 © iStockphoto/jamesbenet; p. 9 Yuttasak Jannarong/Shutterstock.com; pp. 11, 15 Rodney Mehring/Shutterstock.com; p. 13 Scott Camazine/Photo Researchers/Getty Images; p. 17 Lenrer/Shutterstock.com; p. 19 W Treat Davidson/Photo Researchers/Getty Images.

Printed in the United States of America

CPSIA compliance information: Batch #CS16GS: For further information contact Gareth Stevens, New York, New York at 1-800-542-2595.

Contents

Words in the glossary appear in **bold** type the first time they are used in the text.

What's Buzzin'?

There's a killer among us. It lives in our neighborhoods. It attacks at a moment's notice. But this killer isn't a human—it's the killer bee.

The killer bee's deadly **reputation** comes from the very thing that hurts its enemies: its sting! But a single killer bee's sting isn't as bad as it sounds. It's actually how these bees act in a group that makes them seem like killers. Does the killer bee live up to its nasty name? Read on to find out!

Is the killer bee something to be feared, or is it simply misunderstood? You be the judge.

From Faraway Lands

It's likely the bees you're used to seeing are European honeybees. For some time, they were the only kind of honeybees in North America. That all changed about 60 years ago.

In 1956, scientists brought several colonies of African honeybees to Brazil. They wanted to study them more closely. They found that African honeybees and European honeybees were very similar. Scientists wanted to breed, or cross, them. They hoped the new bees would have **traits** of both kinds of bees.

THAT SMARTS!

Scientists thought crossing African honeybees with the honeybees in Brazil would make a new kind of honeybee that produced more honey.

Scientists hoped by crossing the two honeybees, they would create a honeybee with the African honeybee's ability to survive many conditions and the quieter nature of the European honeybee.

The New Bee in Town

Though the African honeybees were much like the European honeybees, scientists had to be careful about bringing an unfamiliar species, or kind, to a new place. They didn't want to bring anything new into the **ecosystem** without knowing what would happen.

Scientists were careful. They tried to keep the African honeybees separate and controlled. But in 1957, several queen bees accidentally escaped. Once they were in the wild, scientists had no way of controlling what the queens would do. The queens **mated** with local bees and produced the first killer bees.

That Smarts!

"Killer bees" is just a nickname. Their scientific name is Apis mellifera scutellanta, and they're commonly called Africanized honeybees.

Brazil's hot weather was perfect for the new kind of bees. It allowed them to live there successfully.

The Bee Body

A killer bee looks like a regular honeybee. It has a head, **thorax**, and **abdomen**. The killer bee's eyes are on its head. Its wings and legs are attached to its thorax. It's almost impossible to tell a killer bee and a regular honeybee apart just by looking at them. You have to look at their **DNA**!

Only female bees have stingers. The stinger is found at the end of the abdomen. Male bees can't sting you. Their only job is to mate with the queen.

THAT SMARTS!

Even though the queen's main job is to lay eggs to keep the hive growing, she has a stinger, too. The queen is commonly the biggest bee in the hive.

Is this bee a male or female? It's female. You know because it has a stinger!

A Venomous Sting

No one wants to get stung by a bee, let alone a killer bee. But believe it or not, a killer bee's sting is no more deadly than a regular bee's.

A bee stings when it feels like it's in danger. It dives at its **target** and pushes its stinger into the skin. Then **venom** flows from the bee's body through the stinger and into its target. Bees don't live long after. They leave the stinger and important body parts behind.

THAT SMARTS!

Bee venom causes pain and itching. It's the bees' way of telling us not to bother them. One bee sting is all it takes to make you stay away in the future.

Bee stingers are pointy and sharp enough to break through human skin.

Bad Bee-havior

It may seem unfair that killer bees have a bad reputation, especially since their stings are the same as any old bee sting. But don't be fooled—their **behavior** is what makes them dangerous.

Killer bees act differently than regular bees. They're known to be very **aggressive**, something they got from the African honeybees they come from. Also like the African honeybee, killer bees are quick to attack. They attack in large numbers. And they don't let their prey get away easily.

THAT SMARTS!

European honeybees don't commonly bother people and often fly away when left alone.

Killer bees respond more strongly and quickly than regular bees do.

Protecting the Hive

Killer bees' aggressive behavior is their way of protecting what matters most to them: their hive. They may think any noise or movement around them is an attempt to hurt their hive.

Killer bees attack in **swarms**, which is one of the most dangerous things about them. Hives can hold as many as 50,000 bees. If they all respond at once, that's a lot of bee stings! People who have been attacked by killer bees have suffered hundreds of stings at the same time.

THAT SMARTS!

Five hundred bee stings hold as much venom as a rattlesnake bite.

Bees protect their hive because the queen bee—the most important bee—lives inside.

The Thrill of the Chase

If you ever come across a killer bee hive, run quickly in the other direction! But even that may not be enough to save you. Killer bees have been known to chase a target for long distances. They can follow people for up to 1/4 mile (0.4 km).

Killer bees have been responsible for hundreds of deaths, but scientists often point out that people can die from any kind of bee sting. So remember, a sting by one killer bee won't kill you—but stings from thousands just might!

That Smarts!

People with bee allergies can be harmed by a single sting from any kind of bee! Their bodies react badly to the venom.

This bee still has its stinger. Maybe it will just fly away!

Bee Careful

Many people are afraid of killer bees. Understanding this stinging creature helps make it less scary! Scientists are looking for ways to reduce the killer bee population so that we don't have to fear them.

It's important to be careful when you're near any bee, not just the killer kind. There are some things you can do to protect yourself. If you see a beehive, leave it alone. Be very quiet and still. Loud noises and quick movements may cause them to swarm!

THAT SMARTS!

Killer bees originated in Brazil, but it didn't take them long to spread out from there. Over the past 60 years, they've made their way through South America and into the southern and western United States.

On the Move

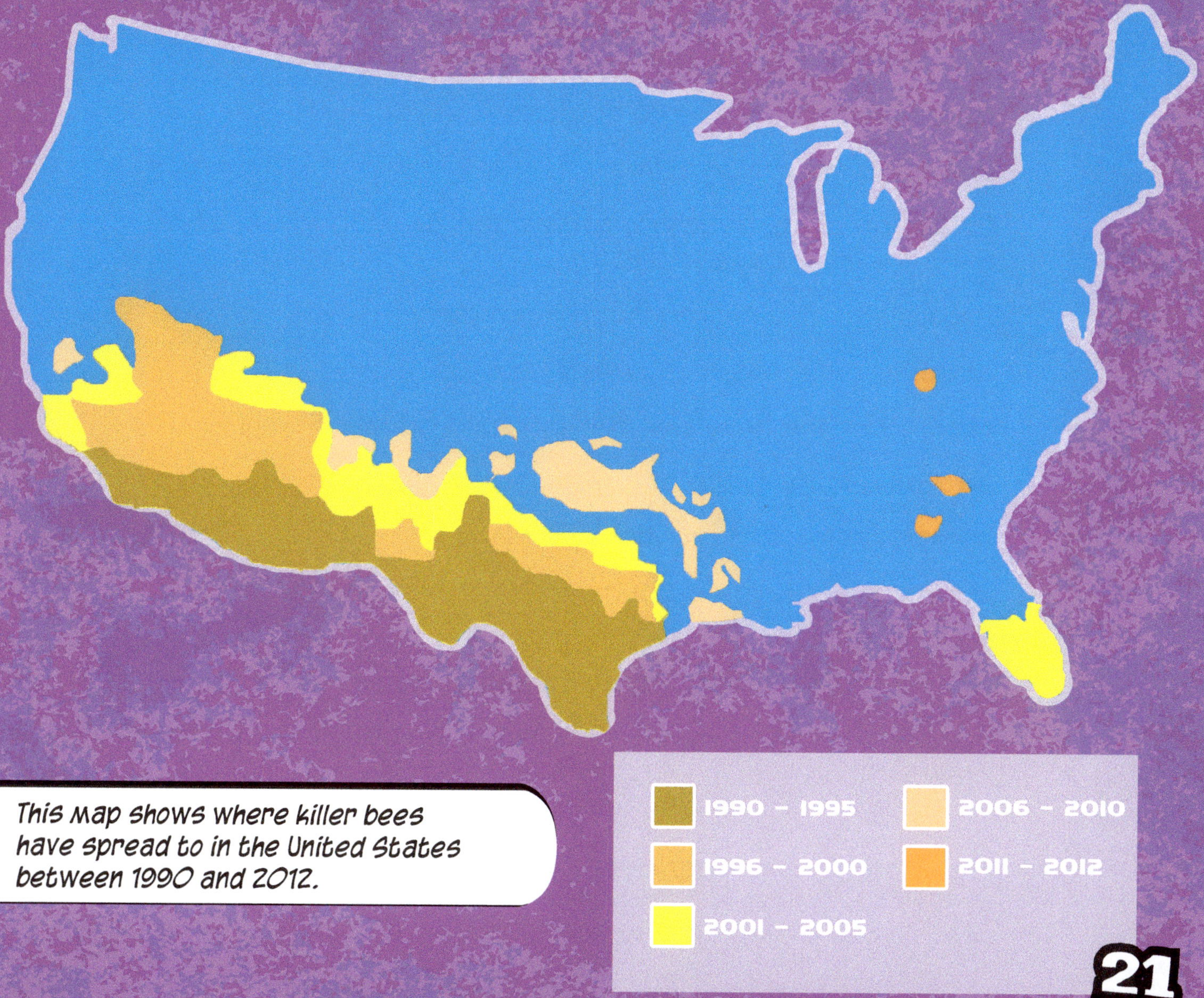

This map shows where killer bees have spread to in the United States between 1990 and 2012.

Glossary

abdomen: the large, rear part of an insect's body

aggressive: ready to fight or attack

behavior: the way of acting

DNA: part of the body that carries genetic information, which gives the instructions for life

ecosystem: all the living things in an area

mate: to come together to make babies

reputation: the beliefs or opinions held about something

swarm: a large group of insects, especially flying ones

target: the focus of an attack

thorax: the middle part of an insect's body. The wings and legs connect to it.

trait: a feature that is passed on from parents to children

venom: something an animal makes in its body that can harm other animals

For More Information

Books

Owings, Lisa. *Killer Bees*. Minneapolis, MN: Bellwether Media, 2013.

Winters, Kari-Lynn. *Buzz About Bees*. Markham, ON: Fitzhenry & Whiteside, 2013.

Websites

Bee Facts for Kids
kids.sandiegozoo.org/animals/insects/bee
Learn many facts about bees through this website, created and managed by the San Diego Zoo.

Killer Bees (or Africanized Honeybees)
www.exploringnature.org/db/detail.php?dbID=11&detID=118
This website provides lots of important information on killer bees.

Publisher's note to educators and parents: Our editors have carefully reviewed these websites to ensure that they are suitable for students. Many websites change frequently, however, and we cannot guarantee that a site's future contents will continue to meet our high standards of quality and educational value. Be advised that students should be closely supervised whenever they access the Internet.

Index